SIMPLE CLOTH DAISY DOLLS

WENCHE O. STEENSEN

Photography by **Claus Dalby**

Search Press

First published in Great Britain in 2014 by Search Press Limited,
Wellwood, North Farm Road, Tunbridge Wells, Kent, TN2 3DR

Reprinted 2014

The original Danish edition was published as *Tusindfryd-Dukker*.

This edition is published by arrangement with Claudia Böhme Rights & Literary Agency, Hannover, Germany (www.agency-boehme.com).

English translation by Burravoe Translation Ltd.

ISBN: 978-1-84448-929-9

Printed in China

CONTENTS

THE STORY BEHIND THE DAISY DOLL

I have always loved dolls and have enjoyed playing with them since I was very young. My childhood world was filled with dolls of all different sizes, colours and materials. For me they meant security, friendship, role-play and the development of imagination. I clung to the world of dolls until the age of twelve. After that came a long break, during which all my doll children remained safe and sound in my grandmother's display cabinet.

When my first child, a daughter, came into the world, my doll life began to flourish again. I wanted to pass on my love of dolls to my daughter. I felt that her first doll should be soft and warm, have a personality and be filled with kind thoughts and love, and it should not contain any harmful substances, so I could safely leave the two of them arm in arm.

I searched far and wide for techniques and materials. I tried out proportions, changed and adjusted shapes – and changed them again. Over the course of eighteen months I developed my own procedure and the characteristic pattern of the Daisy Doll.

The first Daisy Doll, along with a suitcase of dolls' clothes, became my daughter's present on her second birthday. Since then I have had the privilege of making dolls for children in many different places all over the globe. The doll world of my childhood has been the starting point for many creative years of adult life.

I hope that this book will inspire, motivate and guide mothers, sisters, grandparents and others interested in dolls to make their very own doll for a very special person.

Enjoy!
Wenche

DAISY DOLLS

The dolls in this book are 40–45cm (16–18in) high – a good size for children of all ages. Their expressions and facial features are very basic because the more simply the doll is shaped, the more it stimulates the child's own imagination.

body materials

I use only natural materials for the dolls: 100% cotton tubular gauze for the inner head and upper body; 100% cotton doll-making jersey-knit fabric for the doll's skin, and washed, carded sheep's wool for stuffing. See page 15 for further details.

I stuff the dolls with wool because, when firmly stuffed, wool has a certain elasticity that makes the doll firm and soft at the same time. Wool is also self-cleaning and feels warm to the touch, so it makes a soft, warm doll to hold in your arms.

The eyes and mouth are embroidered with embroidery cotton of various kinds. All types of yarn can be used for the hair, and each yarn will create a look of its own.

clothing

At the end of the book (see page 55) there are some basic patterns for clothing to fit the dolls, including dresses, shirts, blouses, trousers and pinafores. These are all very easy to make.

For those experienced in the art of sewing, the patterns can provide a starting point for major or minor adjustments, embellished with a sprinkling of imagination.

water and washing

A cloth doll is obviously not suitable for repeated play in the bath, but a much-loved and played-with doll will inevitably attract one or two dirty spots. I think most spots should be seen as the natural patina of age and a sign that the doll has life around it.

However, if the dolls get dirty, you can easily treat the marks by using a mild, colourless soap to lather the area and then rinse it under lukewarm running water. If the doll is so dirty that washing is essential, wash it like a woollen sweater: warm hand wash and dry flat.

BEFORE YOU START

Before getting started on your doll, you should think carefully about the doll's future owner. What needs should the doll fulfil, and what do you wish for the doll's new owner? The recipient's age is also important.

Very small children often use the doll as a dear friend, someone to snuggle up to, while older children begin to investigate fantasy through play, either alone or with other children. Older children like dressing and undressing dolls.

With small children, pay particular attention to the accessories you give the doll, making sure there are no small items like buttons that can be pulled off and swallowed and that the clothes are easy to put on and take off. For older children and adults you can really go to town in the matter of clothes and accessories. You can also adapt the choice of fabrics for the clothes to suit the child's age. If the clothes need to be washable, it is best to use cotton, but if the doll is going to be mainly for decoration, even the most delicate fabrics can be utilised.

the doll's proportions

If the height of the head is 1 unit, the height of the body should be 1.5 units and the length of the arms and legs 1.5 units. When the arms have been sewn in place, the hands should reach to about the height of the doll's hips.

Once you have had a little practice, you can make your own adaptations to the doll pattern in this book. Then you can take your doll-making further by adding your own details and adjustments to the pattern.

The measurements given in this book are guidelines, in the sense that they must always be adapted to the individual doll. Natural materials are 'living' and therefore work in different ways. In addition, the final measurements will always depend on how firmly the doll is stuffed.

REQUIREMENTS

 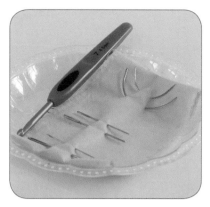

sewing accessories

pins
– these should be long and strong with big round heads, plus you will need ordinary round-headed pins.

doll needle
– this is an extra-long, strong needle.

ordinary, strong sewing needles
– sharps and blunts.

curved needle

thimble
– this is indispensable!

tape measure

chalk pencil

scissors

sewing machine
– preferably one that can sew stretch stitch.

crochet hook
– medium size.

narrow smooth tube
– about 20cm (8in) long and 3cm (1¼in) in diameter to help with stuffing. You can make a stuffing pipe from a sheet of plastic laminate or similar rolled up and taped in place.

large, strong knitting needle
– with a rounded tip, e.g. 6mm (US size 10/ UK size 4), to help turn the pieces out and for pushing in the wadding.

materials for doll making

tubular gauze
– for the inner head and upper body.
For one doll you need about 50cm
(20in).

jersey knit doll fabric
– for the skin of the doll, use high-quality interlock cotton double-jersey stockinette fabric.
I use Ekotex Standard 100, which
is easy to clean, wear-resistant
and keeps its shape well, but you
could use any high-quality doll-skin
fabric suitable for Waldorf/Steiner
dolls. I prefer to use one type for
faces, which is soft and stretchy and
therefore clings nicely to the details
of the face, and a firmer, more
tightly knitted body fabric to help
ensure that the doll will not become
floppy and lose its shape after
a time.

string thread
– suitable for crafting, which should
be a strong, non-fraying variety.

wool for stuffing
– which should be washed, carded
sheep's wool. This is available
from doll-making, spinning and
felting suppliers.

embroidery thread
– in the colours of the eyes and
mouth. I recommend DMC cotton
embroidery thread. It is good quality,
does not easily knot when you need
to sew through the doll's head many
times, and comes in a wide range
of colours.

sewing thread
– in the colours of the skin and hair.

knitting yarn
– for the doll's hair. The yarns that
give the most natural-looking
hair are mohair yarns with a high
percentage of wool, both smooth
and bouclé. Ordinary wool gives fine,

straight hair. It is also very suitable
for dolls for small children, as it is
very wear-resistant. Alpaca yarn
gives you a happy medium between
the previous two.

blusher (rouge)
– for the cheeks.

materials for the clothes and accessories

cotton fabrics

sewing thread

stretch lace elastic trim
– for decoration and edgings.

elastic

Petersham ribbon

felt balls
– for the hair band.

old-fashioned buttons
– which can be bought from
flea markets or salvaged from old
clothes.

press studs

cotton yarn
– for the crocheted hat.

MAKING THE DOLL'S HEAD

making the inner head

1. Prepare about 50cm (20in) of tubular gauze, 4cm (1½in) wide, by tacking it together at one end. Tie firmly about 0.5cm (¼in) from the end (see photo 1).

2. Roll up the tubular gauze, ready to unroll it right side out (photo 2). Set aside ready for use.

3. Take two smoothed strips of wool stuffing, which are not too thick and are about 20 x 45cm (8 x 18in). Lay them in a cross-shape and leave ready to use, as shown in photo 3. Now pull off about ten strips of stuffing, about 10 x 40cm (4 x 16in). These strips must not be too thick. Leave these ready to use as well.

4. Take a nice big handful of stuffing. Warm it in your hands and begin shaping it into a ball. Continue until you have made a firm ball (photo 4).

5. Take the ten strips of stuffing, one at a time, and roll them round the ball, using the 'snowball' method. Roll and turn around, taking care all the time that the growing ball remains firm (photos 5–10).

6. Continue until the ball is about 32cm (12½in) in circumference (photo 11).

7. Shape the ball (see photo 12).

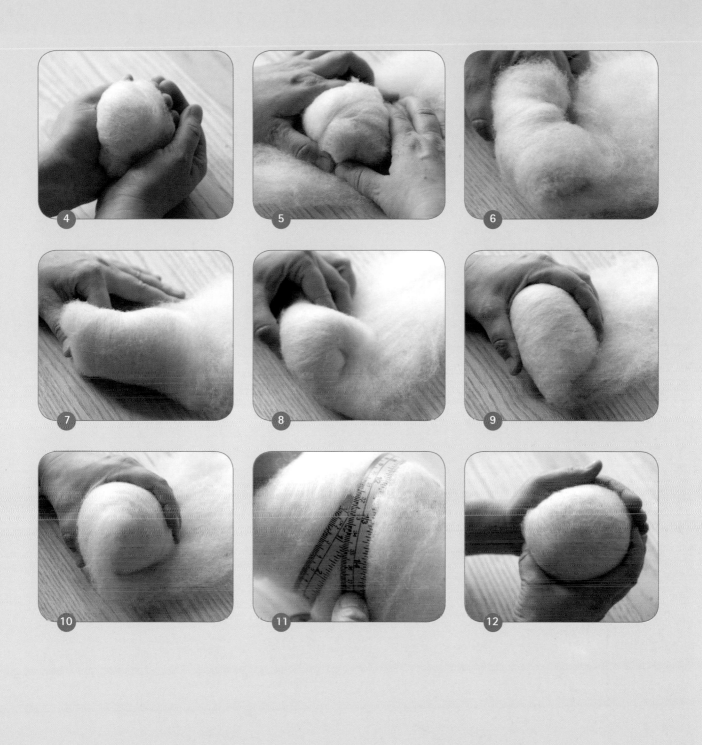

8. Now position the ball in the middle of the cross of stuffing you prepared in step 3 (photo 13). Keep a firm grip on the ball all the time so it remains firm.

9. Turn the whole arrangement over, so the cross is on top, keeping hold of the ball with one hand and holding the cross on top of it with the other (photo 14). Press the ball down on the table and use both hands to fold the 'arms' of the cross down around the ball.

10. Bring the arms of the cross together in a firm grip underneath the ball (photo 15). This area, directly under the ball, will become the doll's neck, and the wadding below that will become the top of the body.

11. Keep a tight hold on the wadding while you pick up the gauze with your other hand and hold it just above the ball, as shown in photo 16. Grasp the ball as far down as you can and pull the gauze down over it (photo 17).

12. Push the rest of the stuffing into the gauze tube. Pull the gauze down tight over it and tie off with string. Tie a bow here so it can easily be undone later (photo 18). A hint of the neck can be seen between the head and the upper body. Put your hands round the neck and press in a little to make it more obvious.

13. The head should now measure about 10cm (4in) from the top to the neck when measured straight (see the illustration top right and photo 19).

14. Tie the neck with string – wind the string twice round the neck and tie a firm knot (photos 20–24). A reef knot makes a good locking knot (see the second illustration, right). This string marks the neck line.

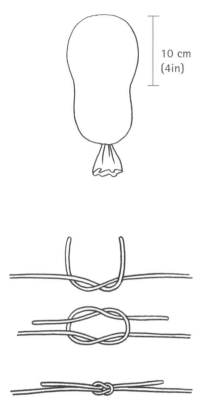

10 cm (4in)

Reef knot

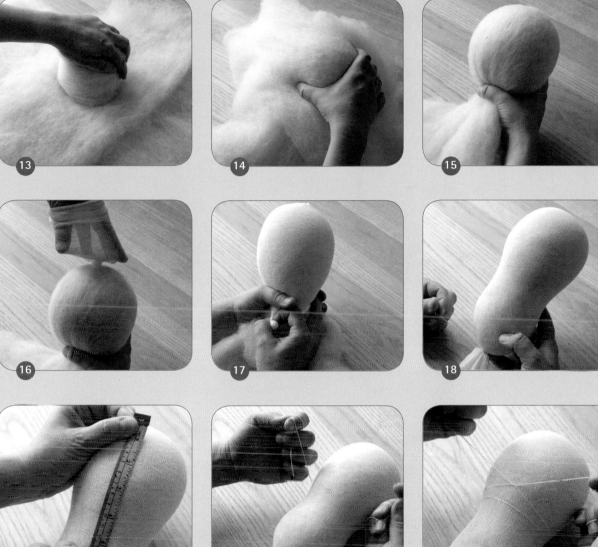

marking the eye line

1. The eyes are always in the middle of the face. For a head measuring 10cm (4in), the eye line will be 5cm (2in) down from the top of the head. Measure 5cm (2in) from the top of the head in about four places and make a horizontal mark for the eye line using chalk pencil or dressmaker's temporary fabric marker (photo 25).

2. Take a piece of string about 150cm (60in) long, find the middle and press it against the eye line along the 5cm (2in) marks. Wind the string twice around the inner head, as shown in photos 26–27.

3. Pull the string tight to make a clear indentation about 0.5cm (¼in) deep all the way round (photos 28–29). Tie with a reef knot as before (see page 22).

4. Push a long, strong pin into the knot point (photo 30). This is the first of two eye-line knots.

5. Measure the circumference at the eye line and insert another strong pin on the opposite side, exactly halfway round (photo 31). This is the second eye-line knot. Before going any further, hold the head a little way away from you to make sure the eye line is at the same height all the way round.

6. At the first eye-line knot there are two ends of string. Bring one over the top of the head to the pin on the other side and continue on under the 'chin' and back up to the first pin (photos 32–34).

7. Pull the string tight and wind it round again. Tie a reef knot by the pin (photo 35).

8. Fasten the crossed strings firmly in place by sewing a cross over the eye-line knots (photo 36).

shaping the cheeks

1. From the front, the head should look as shown in photo 37, and from the side as shown in photo 38. The string that goes down around the chin is the front cheek line (see the illustration below).

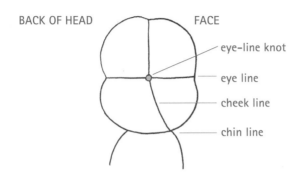

BACK OF HEAD   FACE

eye-line knot

eye line

cheek line

chin line

2. At the pin in one eye-line knot there are two ends of string. Using the long doll needle, pull one end straight through the head to the pin on the opposite side. Fasten the crossing strings with a stitch as you did in step 8 on page 24 (see photos 39–40).

3. Using a crochet hook, pull the eye line at the back of the head right down to the chin line. Take care not to tear holes in the fine gauze with the crochet hook, so always keep the point of the hook turned outwards towards you (photos 41–42). You should now have a triangle of string (see photo 43).

4. The string at the front of the triangle is the front cheek line and the string at the back (which was previously the eye-line string from the back of the head) is now the back cheek line. 'Close' this triangle by sewing the two strings (cheek lines) together to create the doll's round cheeks. To do this, thread a strong, blunt needle with the remaining string from the eye-line knot and sew the front and back cheek lines together without pushing the needle into the gauze. Work all the way down to the neck line and fasten off firmly by sewing a few stitches into the thread of the neck line (see photos 44–45). Repeat this step on the other side.

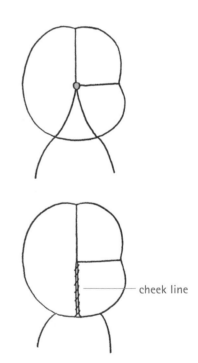

cheek line

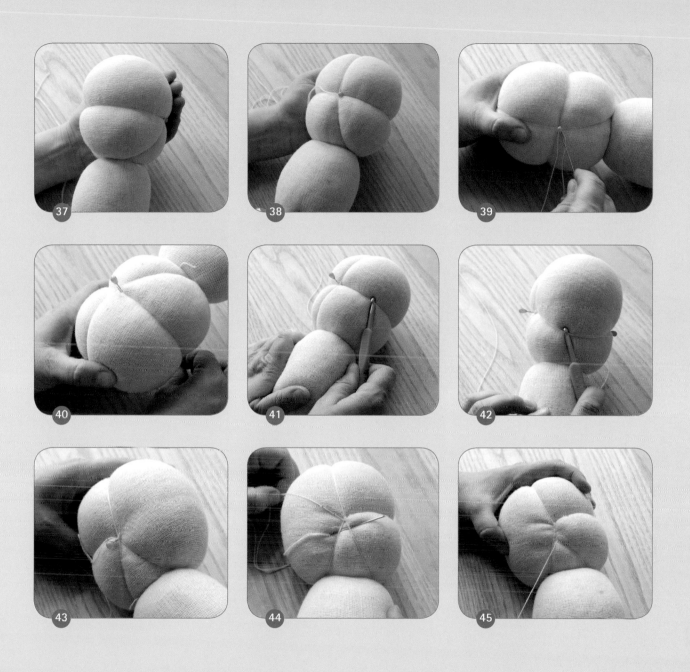

adding the skin

1. Take a piece of the knit fabric for the face 40cm (16in) wide and 35cm (14in) high and fold it so it measures 20 x 35cm (8 x 14in). Pay attention to the direction of the grain: the 'stripes' of the fabric should run parallel to the fold.

2. Place the head on the fabric with the face towards the fold, so it projects about 0.5cm (¼in) beyond the folded edge. With a chalk pencil, draw the outline of the head from the forehead round to the back of the neck and upper body and then continue straight down the whole length of the fabric (photo 46).

3. Sew along the outline, preferably using a stretch stitch. (Zigzag will work if your machine does not do a specialist stretch stitch.) Cut out, leaving a seam allowance of about 0.5cm (¼in). Clip the fabric in the seam allowance towards the seam, all the way round the curve of the head and neck, taking care not to cut the stitches (photo 47).

4. Turn right side out (photo 48).

5. Place the head on the table with the face side uppermost. Pull the face fabric down over the head so the seam runs straight down the middle of the back of the head. Make sure the back of the neck fits snugly (photo 49).

6. Tie string around the neck line, taking care that the skin does not form folds (photos 50–51).

Note: it is best to embroider the face after you have finished making the doll (see page 39).

MAKING THE BODY

cutting and sewing the body pieces

1. First trace the pattern pieces for the body, arms and legs from pages 70–71 on to card to make templates. You can use these over and over again.

2. Cut two pieces of the thick body fabric 20cm (8in) wide and 30cm (12in) high with the grain running lengthways, i.e. so the 'stripes' run down the length of the fabric. Place the pieces right sides together, with the 'stripes' matching. On the upper piece, make a horizontal pleat about 1.5cm (½in) deep as marked on the pattern and shown in the first illustration, right. Secure it with pins. Position the body pattern so the broken lines lie along the folds (photo 52). The pleat is where the legs will later be sewn in.

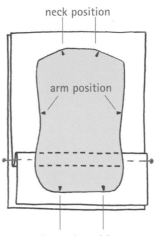

neck position

arm position

buttock position

3. Using the chalk pencil, draw around the edge of the pattern (without adding any seam allowance) and mark the pattern's positioning points on both sides for the neck, arms and buttocks, as shown in the illustrations.

4. Cut two pieces of the thick body fabric 40cm (16in) wide and 30cm (12in) high and place them right sides together. Arrange the pattern pieces for the arms and legs parallel to the grain as shown in photo 53. As before, draw around the edges of the patterns without adding a seam allowance.

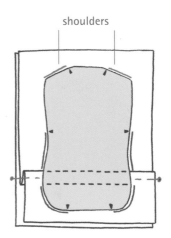

shoulders

5. Sew the body pieces together using a stretch stitch along the chalk line from each arm marker down to the top of the pleat and from the bottom of the pleat down to the buttock markers, as indicated by the blue lines in the second illustration. Cut out the body about 0.5cm (¼in) from the seam. Clip into the seam allowances at the curves and notches. Insert pins at the arm markers (photo 54).

6. Sew around each arm and leg, along the chalk line, using a stretch stitch and leaving the short, straight edge open for turning. Cut out each piece and clip the seam allowances at all the curves and notches, for instance at the thumb, back of the knee and instep, as you did for the body (photo 55).
7. Turn the arms and legs right side out. A knitting needle with a rounded point is useful to help get the thumbs fully turned out (photo 56).

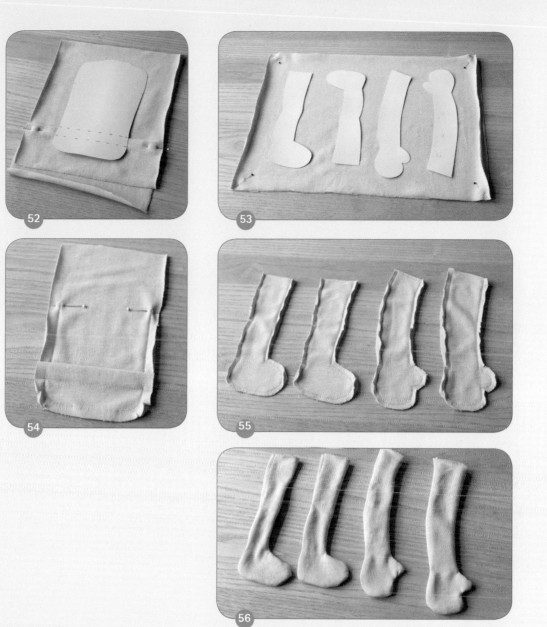

stuffing the limbs

It is best if you prepare the stuffing to be used for both arms and both legs at the start. Make sure you have the same amount for each part. It is easier if you stuff, say, both arms at the same time, because once the wool has been pushed into the fabric, you will not be able to remember how much you used.

1. Lay out your stuffing. For each upper limb, you will need a little tuft for the thumb, an oval ball for the hand and a roll for the arm (photo 57). For each lower limb you will need an oval ball for the foot and a roll for the leg. You will also need the stuffing pipe (see page 13).

2. Start by pushing the little tuft of wool into the thumb of each hand, using a knitting needle with a rounded point to push it into position (photos 58–59). Press firmly into place.

3. Keep a firm grip on the stuffing in the thumb while you push the stuffing pipe right down to the end of the hand (photo 60).

4. Take the oval ball of wool and start by pushing it a little way into the tube with your fingers (photo 61). Next, use the point of the knitting needle to push the ball of stuffing right down into the hand (photo 62). Press the ball in well so the hand becomes firm while at the same time carefully pulling the stuffing tube out a little way.

5. Insert the roll of stuffing for each arm in the same way (photo 63). Make sure the arms are firmly stuffed all the way along. Wool will 'settle', so the arms and legs will get floppy over time if they are not stuffed firmly enough. Leave about 4cm (1½in) of fabric unstuffed at the top of the arm and fasten with a pin to keep the stuffing in place.

6. Stuff each leg with the ball and then the roll as you did for the arms. As before, pin the top to keep the stuffing in place (photo 64).

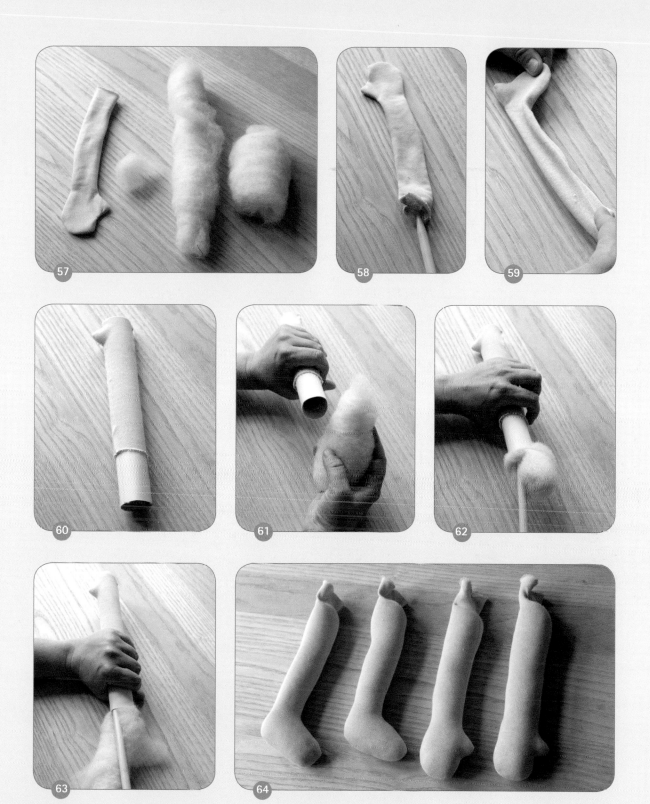

attaching the legs

1. Place the legs on the body pleat so they are symmetrical and preferably about 1cm (½in) apart to allow space for the crotch (see photo 65). Mark their positions using a removable dressmaker's marker and then remove the legs.

2. Cut slits for the legs in between the marks you just made on the body fold (photo 66).

3. Insert the legs from the right side (inside) through the holes in the fold, so the feet end up lying on the shoulder part of the body (see photo 67). Pin the seam allowances of the legs and the body firmly together. Check that the legs are the same length and facing the right way before stitching. Now comes the first really tricky bit of sewing – getting the doll's legs under the sewing machine foot. Sew along the fold, using a stretch stitch and working as close as you can to the stuffed parts of the legs. Be careful not to catch the doll's buttocks in the stitching.

4. Turn the body out and make sure the legs are sewn in correctly (photo 68).

attaching the arms

The arms should be attached so that the hands reach to around the hips, as shown in photo 72. Attach the arms one at a time as follows:

1. Lay the body with the front upwards. Fold the front part down to the two pins and then position one of the arms so it is level with the edge of the shoulder, as shown in photo 69.

2. Attach the unstuffed fabric of the arm to the seam allowance of the body as tightly as you can, and sew from the neck marker to the arm marker using a stretch stitch to join the front, back and arm together. (These marks are shown in the illustrations on page 30 and given on the body pattern.) Repeat to attach the second arm (photo 70). Of course, this will be trickier, now that the first arm has been sewn in. You may, perhaps, prefer to sew in the second arm with hand stitching.

3. Check that your doll looks as shown in photos 71–73. The body, arms and legs are now joined together. Only the seams at the neck and buttocks still remain to be sewn.

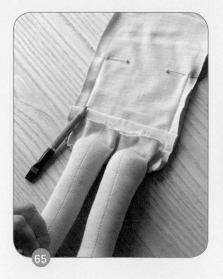

65

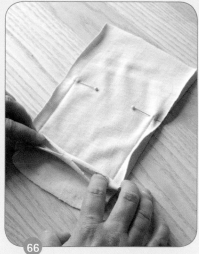

66

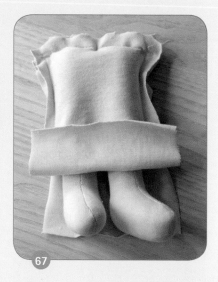

67

68

69

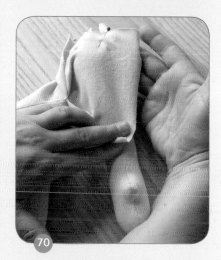

70

71

72

73

attaching the head

1. Untie the string at the bottom of the head section (see photo 18, page 23) and loosen the stuffing. If necessary, take out just enough stuffing to enable everything to pass through the neck opening on the body. Push your hand through the body from the buttocks and up through the neck opening (photo 74).

2. Grasp the head section and pull through the neck opening until the neck line reaches the neck opening on the body (photo 75). Pin the neck opening of the body firmly around the neck line and then fill the body with stuffing until it feels firm and even.

3. On each side of the doll there is now about 1cm (½in) of shoulder seam still open (photo 76). These two seams must be sewn up to the neck line with an invisible seam. Turn under the seam allowances on these seams. Thread a strong, short, sharp needle with a double length of flesh-coloured sewing thread. Sew up the seams by taking small stitches through alternate edges, starting each stitch level with where you took the needle out on the opposite side (ladder stitch – see the illustrations). When the thread is pulled tight, the two folded edges will come together and the stitching will be invisible (photo 77). If you are unsure about working this stitch, practise first on two scraps of folded fabric.

4. Continue sewing around the entire neck opening in the same way (photo 78). Keep the stitches in the folded edge of the body and a little way down into the neck line so that the opening is fastened to the neck. Pull the thread tight enough so the neck opening sits evenly along the neck line on the head, but not so tight that the fabric puckers (photo 79). This is where practice makes perfect!

5. You are almost at the end. Turn the buttocks towards you (photo 80). Add extra stuffing until the whole body is firmly filled right down to the buttocks. Carefully trim away any superfluous tubular gauze from the bottom of the head section. Fold the edges of the knitted fabric to the inside at the opening to give two neatly folded edges of the same length.

6. Join the folded edges together along the buttocks using a short, strong needle and double flesh-coloured thread. Once again, use an invisible stitch such as ladder stitch (photo 81).

7. The doll's body is finished. Check that it is firmly stuffed and neatly sewn up, with no stitches visible on the outside (photo 82).

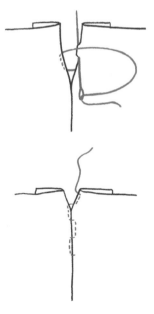

ladder stitch

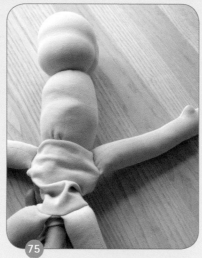

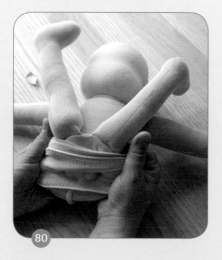

ADDING THE FACIAL FEATURES

stitching the eyes and mouth

1. To find the best position for the eyes and mouth, insert three pins in an equilateral triangle, as shown in photo 83. To do this, first find the midpoint between the two eye-line knots. This is the centre of the face. Insert a guiding pin here.

2. Measure 3cm (1¼in) out from each side along the eye line and insert a green-headed pin.

3. Insert a red-headed pin about 3.5cm (1½in) below the guiding pin and then remove the guiding pin.

4. Now have a good look at the doll. Does the face look well proportioned? If necessary, move the red mouth pin up or down a little or the green eye pins a bit closer together or further apart. A small change here or there can make a big difference to the expression.

5. Measure about 1.5cm (½in) to each side of the red pin and insert a pink-headed pin. You can make this distance longer or shorter, depending on how wide a mouth you want – how much you want the doll to smile (see the illustration, right).

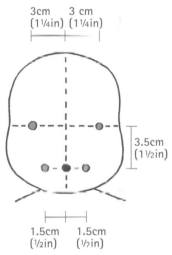

3cm   3 cm
(1¼in) (1¼in)

3.5cm
(1½in)

1.5cm   1.5cm
(½in)   (½in)

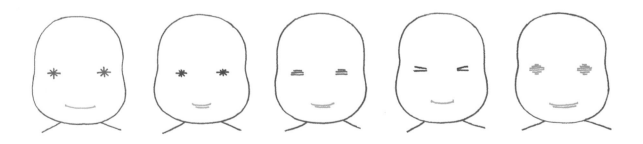

The eyes are embroidered with embroidery cotton. They can easily be made bigger or smaller, narrower or wider by adapting the size of the stitches. I always sew stars for the eyes (see page 40) but perhaps you fancy different eyes. The illustrations above show a few simple alternatives.

embroidering the eyes

1. Thread a long doll needle with three strands of embroidery cotton about 1m (40in) long. Make a knot at the end and pass the needle diagonally through from the top of the head to come out at one of the green-headed pins. (The hair will cover the knot.) The green-headed pin is the midpoint of the eye and you should start and finish at the centre of the eye (photo 84).

2. Change to a short, sharp needle. You will need to make sure that the star eyes are symmetrical on each side of the midpoint. It is a good idea to count the ribs of the fabric and measure the height of the points where the needle goes in and comes out. I make the horizontal stitches go across about 5 ribs and the vertical stitches about 1cm (½in) high. Work the stars as shown in photos 85–90. Take care that the thread does not fray as you stitch and pull the thread through gently so the stitches are firm but do not tear the fabric.

3. After the last stitch of the first eye, change back to the long doll needle and pass the thread through to the other side of the face, coming out at the second green-headed pin (photo 91).

4. Change back to the short, sharp needle and embroider the second eye with the same measurements as the first. Change back to the long doll needle and then pass the thread back up to the top of the head and fasten off (photo 92). The eyes are now finished.

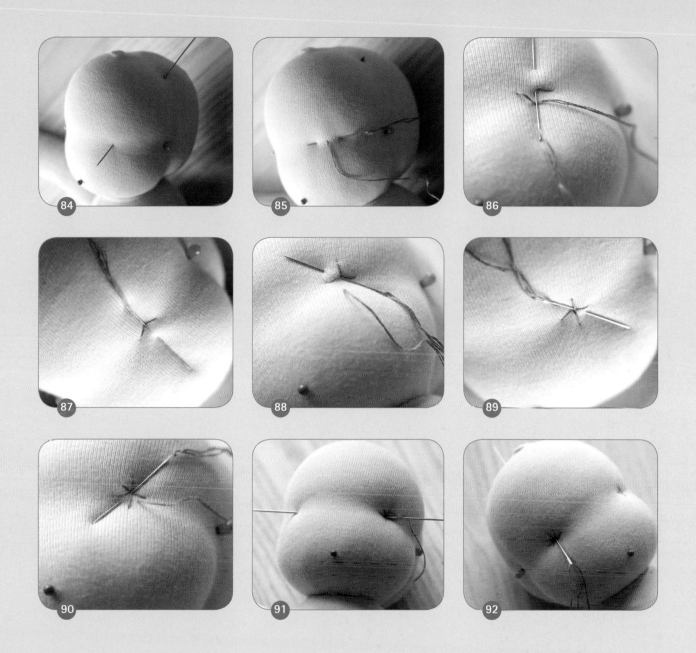

embroidering the mouth

1. Check that the position of the mouth looks right before you begin sewing (photo 93).

2. Thread the long doll needle with six strands of embroidery cotton in your chosen colour and, once again, pass it diagonally through from the top of the head, coming out at one of the pink-headed pins (photo 94). Pull the thread through, but leave an end of about 10cm (4in) hanging loose at the top of the head.

3. Insert the needle at the second pink-headed pin and pass the thread diagonally back up through the head. Take hold of the ends of the thread and pull gently. This will tighten the mouth slightly and produce a little smile (photo 95). When you have decided how much or how little you want the doll to smile, tie the two ends together in a reef knot (see page 22).

colouring the cheeks

Bring the doll to life with rosy cheeks. Use ordinary blusher (rouge) and apply it with a soft brush (photos 96–98). The blusher will gradually fade and will need to be refreshed from time to time. You can also use special wax rouge designed for use on cloth dolls, but this will also need to be reapplied.

93

94

95

96

97

98

ADDING LONG HAIR

I usually give girl dolls a short side parting at the front and then a longer centre parting behind, with bunches or plaits, but all this can be varied as you wish by changing the positioning of the pins. Read through the following before you begin. You will start by using pins to position the yarn for the hair on one half of the head and then stitch it in place before attaching the hair to the other half.

positioning the hair

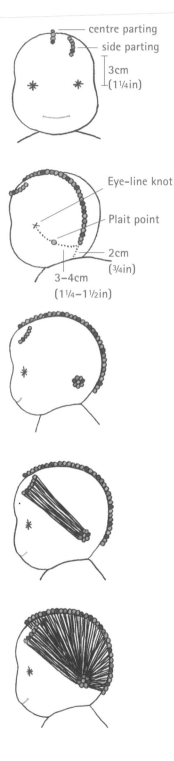

centre parting
side parting
3cm (1¼in)

Eye-line knot
Plait point
2cm (¾in)
3–4cm (1¼–1½in)

1. Insert a straight line of pins running upwards along the line where you want the side parting to go, starting about 3cm (1¼in) above the midpoint of either the right or left eye. Use ordinary round-headed pins, placing them so close together that they touch – about 6 pins in all (see the first illustration, top right).

2. Now find the centre line of the head between the forehead and the nape of the neck by measuring across the head from one eye-line knot to the other in three or four places. Insert pins all the way along this centre line, ending 2cm (¾in) from the nape of the neck.

3. Working from the pin closest to the nape of the neck, measure 3–4cm (1¼–1½in) to each side at a slightly upward angle. Insert a pin. This will be the plait point (see the second illustration).

4. Now make a tight circle of pins around the pin at the plait point, as shown in the third illustration.

5. Position the hair by winding the yarn twice around the pin at the centre of the plait point. Now wind the yarn in figures of eight between the pins at the plait point and the pins along the side parting (and later the centre parting). There should be at least two figures of eight around each pin on the partings to get good coverage over the scalp. Be systematic. Start by going up to the outermost pin of the side parting, come back to the nearest pin at the plait point and continue in the same way round every pin at the side parting. As the pins at the plait point gradually fill up with wool, move on to the next pin in a clockwise direction (see the fourth illustration).

6. Now take the wool around the pins of the centre parting one by one, winding in figures of eight between these and the plait point (see the fifth illustration). When the whole of one side of the doll's head is covered by a nice thick layer of wool and no more of the scalp is visible, wind the yarn twice round the pin at the centre of the plait point and cut off.

sewing the hair in place

Attach the hair with hand stitches as described here, using a short, strong, sharp needle. Choose a sewing thread that is a good match for the hair and use the thread double.

1. Starting at the forehead and sewing through the scalp very close to each pin on the partings, bring the needle up from below and down again through the hair. Take care to catch in all the yarn so as not to leave any loose loops or gaps in the hair. When you have sewn all the way from the forehead to the nape of the neck, fasten off the thread securely.
2. Now you have to sew the plait points. Here it is best to use a smallish curved needle with double thread. Work systematically and take a couple of stitches from below up along a pin. Pull tight and make sure you have caught in all the strands of hair. Work clockwise and make sure that, when you have finished, all the ends are so close together that the scalp cannot be seen.
3. One side of the head is now covered, as shown in the photograph, right. Complete the other half of the hair in the same way.

Girl's hair, showing the partings.

making plaits and bunches

1. The easiest way to make plaits or bunches is to find a hardcover book which has a height that is the same as the length you want the hair to be. Wind the yarn for the hair around the book. You should adapt the number of times you wind it round the book to the thickness of the yarn you have chosen, but 30–50 times is usually about right (see the first illustration, right). Use the same number for each plait.

2. With the yarn still on the book, sew through the yarn along the top edge until you think you have caught it all in. I recommend using a curved needle for this (see the second illustration, right).

3. Cut through the yarn along the bottom of the book. This will give you a bunch to sew straight on to the middle of the plait point.

4. Attach the bunch, sewing through the fabric of the scalp and the hair bunch plenty of times so that the hair can stand up to being pulled. After that, the hair can be plaited.

5. Repeat this process on the opposite side.

Plait/bunch about 25cm (10in) long

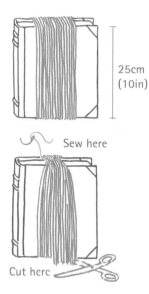

25cm
(10in)

Sew here

Cut here

Extra-thick bunches made of thin alpaca yarn, wound 60 times around a book.

Princess Leia buns. The bunches have been gently knotted to form buns.

Mohair yarn gives the hair a bouffant effect. The yarn for the plaits was wound round a book about 40 times. The ends of the plaits are held in place with small silicon elastic bands, which are child-friendly to take off and put on.

Girl's hair in a wool/silk blend, which makes it look neat. The plaits are thin and the yarn was wound round the book about 30 times.

49

ADDING SHORT HAIR

Short hair looks best if the yarn is applied in two or more layers. The method of application is basically the same as for long hair, but you work from the topmost point of the head instead of from the plait points.

attaching the first layer

1. Start by finding the top point on the head, midway between the eye line at the front and the neck line on the nape of the neck at the back, and midway between the two eye-line knots on the sides of the head. Insert a pin in the top point (see the illustrations below, left and centre).

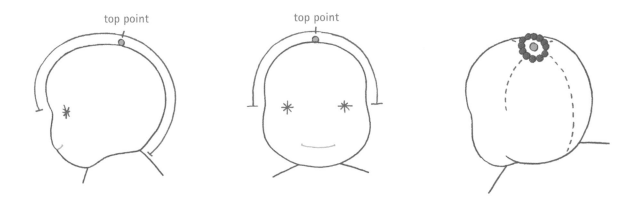

top point   top point

2. Set a circle of pins close together around the top-point pin, about 1.5cm (½in) from the centre pin (see the right-hand illustration, page 50).

3. Insert pins all the way round the head and neck, about 1.5cm (½in) below the desired length of the hair (see the illustration, top right). You could put an elastic band round the head where you want this line to be and insert the pins along it.

4. Remove all the pins. The boy's hair will now consist of a mass of loops that come a little too far down over the eyes and are a bit too long at the back of the neck. You can either leave them like this or cut the loops and trim the hair as desired. You can also add another layer.

attaching the second layer

1. Insert a new ring of pins about 2cm (¾in) below the line you have just sewn, a little lower at the back of the neck than at the forehead, checking the distances all the way round so it is the same on both sides (see the third illustration, right). It is important that the second layer of hair covers the sewing of the first layer (see the bottom illustration, right). To do this, make a circle of pins around the top point closer to the centre pin than before.

2. Wind the yarn in figures of eight as before, so the hair becomes thick and covers the head.

3. Sew down the hair at the pins at the top using a curved needle, and pull tight so the gap at the top is nicely closed up. Sew in a circle all the way round at about 5cm (2in) from the top point (see the fourth illustration, right).

4. Remove all the pins. The boy's hair will now consist of a mass of loops that come a little too far down over the eyes and are a bit too long at the back of the neck. You can either leave them like this or cut the loops and trim the hair as desired. You can also add another layer.

Second line of sewing

First line of sewing

Second layer of hair

First layer of hair

CLOTHING THE DOLLS

Clothes are the key to a world in which you can give free rein to your creativity. The basic patterns on pages 72–77 are for very simple styles, which can be easily adjusted to fit larger or smaller sizes. The patterns are also easy to adapt. Pages 66–69 show just some of the items that you can make. Check the measurements of your own doll before cutting and stitching the fabric.

The choice of fabric must take into account whether the doll will be used mainly for play or for decoration. The clothes in the book are made of cotton fabrics and trimmed with ribbon or stretch lace.

making a dress or blouse

Trace the pattern pieces for the back/front and sleeves from pages 72–73. Fold the fabric and cut two sleeves on the fold, one front on the fold and a pair of back pieces (cut once through both fabric layers). Join the sleeves to the front and back on the sloping seams and then join the underarm/side seams, working with right sides facing and taking a 5mm (¼in) seam allowance. Stitch the centre-back seam from the bottom up to just above halfway so that the garment can be pulled on over the head. Tuck the seam allowance under at the opening and hem (see the photo above centre).

Finish the neck with the neckband. You can use it to make a casing and thread it with elastic. Non-stretch neck edges may be fastened with a button or you can bind the neck with bias binding, leaving long ties at each end to tie in a bow (see the photograph, left). Hem the bottom of the dress or blouse. For sleeve-hem options, see page 56.

making trousers

Trace the pattern pieces for the trousers from pages 74–75 and join them as directed on the patterns. Cut the complete pattern once on folded fabric to make a pair. Fold each piece in half lengthways, right sides together, and stitch the inside-leg seam, then slip one leg inside the other with right sides facing to stitch the crotch seam. Finish the top edge with elastic threaded through a channel.

hemming options

The simplest finish is to fold about 1.5cm (½in) to the wrong side and stitch in place. You can also bind the edges or add a lace trim. To give the sleeves or trousers a puffy shape, you can either thread elastic through a channel or sew on stretch lace using a zigzag stitch (see the photographs below).

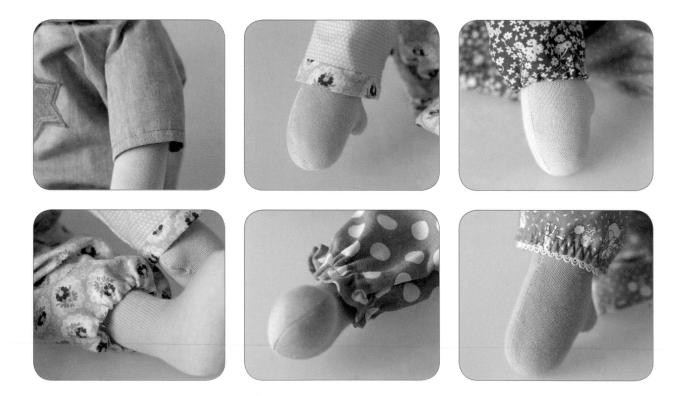

making the blouse and jumpsuit set

The jumpsuit is made without straps so it is easy for little hands to dress the doll. However, for older girls, you can, of course, choose to make straps for it using the pattern on page 77.

Use the pattern on pages 74–75 to make the jumpsuit. Make the broad frill at the top by sewing a channel about 4cm (1½in) from the top edge and threading it with elastic. Stitch a channel at the bottom of the legs and thread with elastic as well.

The blouse can be quite short (see page 66) and is decorated with edging bands in the same fabric as the jumpsuit. Alternatively, you could use a co-ordinating wide bias binding.

making the crocheted hat

This hat is easy to make and lots of fun. It is decorated with three felted wool balls, but you could also use items such as flowers, ribbons and beads – whatever you fancy. However, for very small children you should avoid decorations that could be pulled off.

Because the dolls are handmade, the dimensions of the head may vary a little. The choice of yarn for the hair, in particular, can make a difference to the circumference. The instructions given here are for a doll with a head size of 33cm (13in) and the hat is 10cm (4in) high.

Yarn: Havblik 100% cotton no. 8 (or similar sport-weight/crochet cotton)
Crochet Hook: 3.5cm (UK 9, US E/4)

stitches

The hat is worked in single crochet (UK double crochet), which is abbreviated to sc (UK dc). Increase by crocheting two single crochets (2sc/UK 2dc) into the same stitch (st). Increases should be distributed evenly over the rounds.

Chain 4 stitches and fasten into a ring with a slip stitch.
Round 1: Work 6sc (UK dc) into the ring.
Round 2: Work 2sc (UK dc) in each st around [12 sts].
Rounds 3–5: Increase 6 sts, evenly spaced, in each of the next 3 rounds [30 sts].
Rounds 6–12: Increase 5 sts, evenly spaced, in each of the next 7 rounds [65 sts].
Rounds 13–15: Increase 3 sts, evenly spaced, in each of the next 3 rounds [74 sts].

Rounds 16–24: Work 9 rounds without increasing.
Rounds 25–26 (frill): Work 2sc (UK dc) in every 3rd st of the next 2 rounds [130 st].
Round 27–28: Work 2 rounds without increasing, perhaps in a different colour.
Break off the yarn and fasten off the ends. Trim the hat as desired.

adding appliqué decorations

Clothes for boy dolls can be decorated with simple appliqués. The star template on page 73 can be used to cut a fabric star to stitch to the centre-front of a shirt. In the example shown above, and on page 66, the star was stitched in place using red thread, with two rows of pale stitching inside.

luggage label

A luggage label can be attached to a doll-sized suitcase for a personalised touch. Cut a piece of decorative cotton fabric 18 x 22cm (7 x 8¾in). Fold it in half, with right sides facing, to make a piece 18 x 11cm (7 x 4 ½in) and stitch the edges, taking a 1cm (½in) seam allowance and leaving one short edge open. Turn out, tuck in the raw edges and slip in the ends of a ribbon and carabiner hook. Topstitch securely. Use letter stamps and textile printing powder to stamp the name on some fairly plain cotton fabric and trim to measure 6 x 10cm (2½ x 4in). Stitch this centrally on top of your label. You will need an iron to fix the printing.

an extra suitcase

Older girls might like having an extra suitcase filled with balls of wool, knitting needles or a crochet hook, so they can make something like a scarf for the doll themselves.

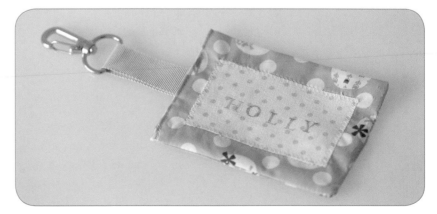

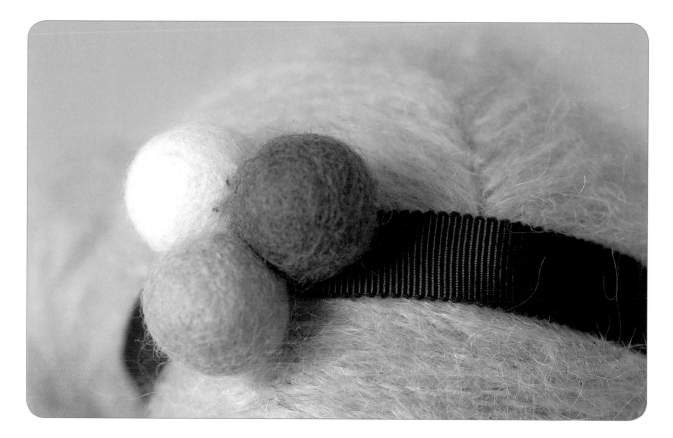

hair band

A hair band is a simple accessory that adds a pretty finishing touch. Use a length of
satin or grosgrain ribbon decorated with felt balls or other simple trimmings. Measure
the circumference of the head and cut the ribbon to fit, allowing a little extra for an
overlap. The hair band can be fastened with a press-stud.

personalised belongings

Adding a label to the doll's personal items is a nice touch. Use letter stamps and textile printing powder as you did for the luggage label (page 62) or use a computer and printer to print on to suitable fabric or fabric-transfer paper. Stitch the finished label to bedding, clothing or accessories.

This nightdress is made using the pattern on pages 72–73. If you would like to make a longer nightdress, simply measure your own doll and see how much the pattern needs to be lengthened.

TOPS AND BLOUSES

The blouse pattern is given on pages 72–73. It has straight sides and can be easily shortened or lengthened, while the sleeve comes in three different lengths. Here are a few examples of the styles you can make.

for a boy

This simple short-sleeved top is shown on page 18. There is a back-neck opening (see page 55), which provides plenty of room to get the top over the doll's head. The neck opening can be fastened with a button or a press-stud. For the appliquéd star, see page 61.

cropped top with frilled sleeves

These sleeves are cut a little wider than on the pattern and the blouse is quite short, as it is to be worn under a pinafore as shown in the photograph on page 52. The frilly cuffs are made by sewing with elastic 2cm (¾in) from the bottom edge. The neck is finished with a band of contrasting fabric that has been threaded with elastic cord (see page 45).

cropped top with contrast bands

This top is trimmed with contrast bands on the long sleeves and neck to match the coordinating jumpsuit (see page 59). The neckband was sewn on to make a channel and threaded with elastic cord and there is an opening at the back of the neck to make it easy to get the blouse over the doll's head (see pages 48–49).

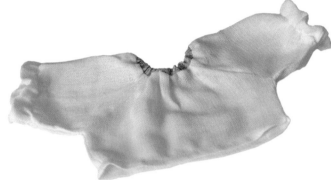

blouse with back necktie

Here, the neck was gathered up slightly with a gathering thread and then trimmed with bias binding, allowing an extra 18cm (7in) of binding at each end for ties (see the photo on page 54). The sleeves and lower edge are gathered by stitching a channel about 2cm (¾in) from the fabric edge and threading it with elastic.

DRESS STYLES

The dress pattern is given on pages 72–73. It uses the same sleeve pattern as the blouse but the body of the dress has slightly flared sides and it can be cut to different lengths.

shirt dress

This short dress (also shown on page 19) has three-quarter-length sleeves. There are channels at the neck and the ends of the sleeves – nice, simple puff sleeves.

dress with elasticated gathers

A lace trim and zigzagging with fine shirring elastic at the wrist add a very pretty, feminine finish (see the detail on page 56). The neck elastic is threaded through a casing (see the photo on page 16).

long-sleeved dress

A short or mid-length dress looks cute worn with three-quarter-length trousers or harem pants (see page 68) as shown in the photo on page 6.

nightdress

Lengthen the dress pattern – measure on your own doll to see how much to add. This nightdress has three-quarter-length sleeves and a non-stretch neckline. See the photos on pages 64 and 65.

TROUSER VARIATIONS

The trouser pattern is given on pages 74–75. To help distinguish between the front and back, sew a cross or length of tape at the top of the back of the trousers. All the designs shown have elastic at the waist.

harem pants

Make the frilled edges by turning over about 3cm (1¼in) and sewing a channel 2–2.5cm (¾–1in) in from the folded edge. Use the pattern for long trousers. Team with a shirt dress (see the photo on page 6).

long gathered trousers

Make channels on the top edge and at the trouser hems and thread with elastic. These trousers look good with a long blouse as shown in the photo on page 60

three-quarter-length trousers

For a young doll or for summer wear, make shorter trousers like these with channels for elastic at the waist and at the bottom hems, as shown in the photos on pages 9 and 19.

straight trousers

These trousers, with elastic at the waist and simple bottom hems, suit boy dolls (see the photo on page 18). Vary the length as desired.

bloomers

These are made from the trouser pattern but with very short legs and a high waist. They look great teamed with short or mid-length dresses (see page 57) or can be worn as underwear.

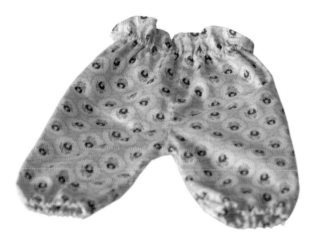

jumpsuit

This model has a high bodice and the frill at the top is extra-wide (see pages 48–49 and 58–59). For older children the jumpsuit can also be made with straps using the pattern on page 77.

PINAFORE

This simple garment can be made with or without straps using the pattern on pages 76–77. It is shown on pages 11 and 49. It can be worn with a short blouse or on its own as a sundress.

PATTERNS

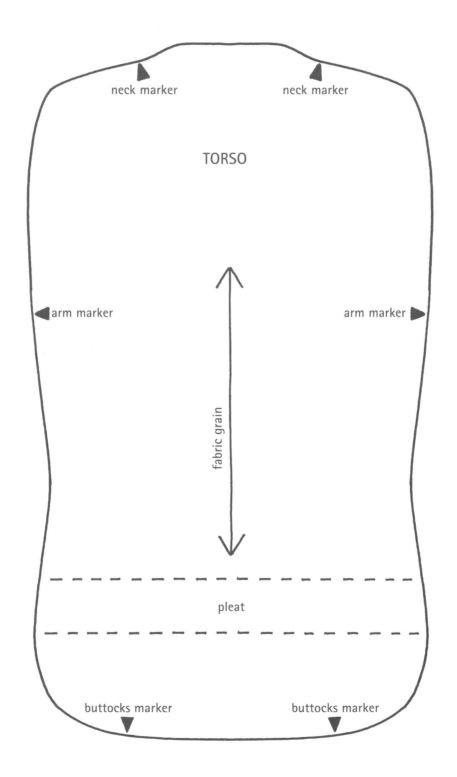

TORSO

neck marker · neck marker

arm marker · arm marker

fabric grain

pleat

buttocks marker · buttocks marker

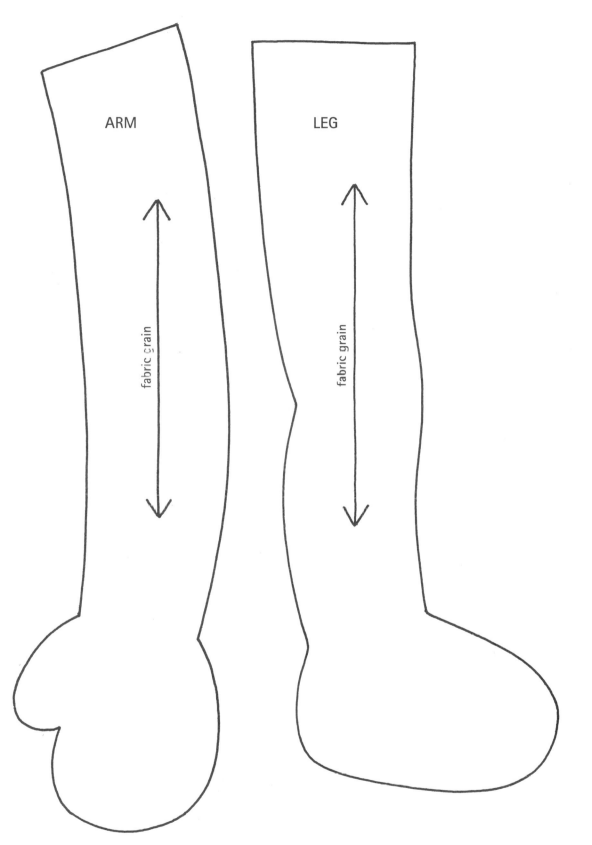

ARM

LEG

fabric grain

fabric grain

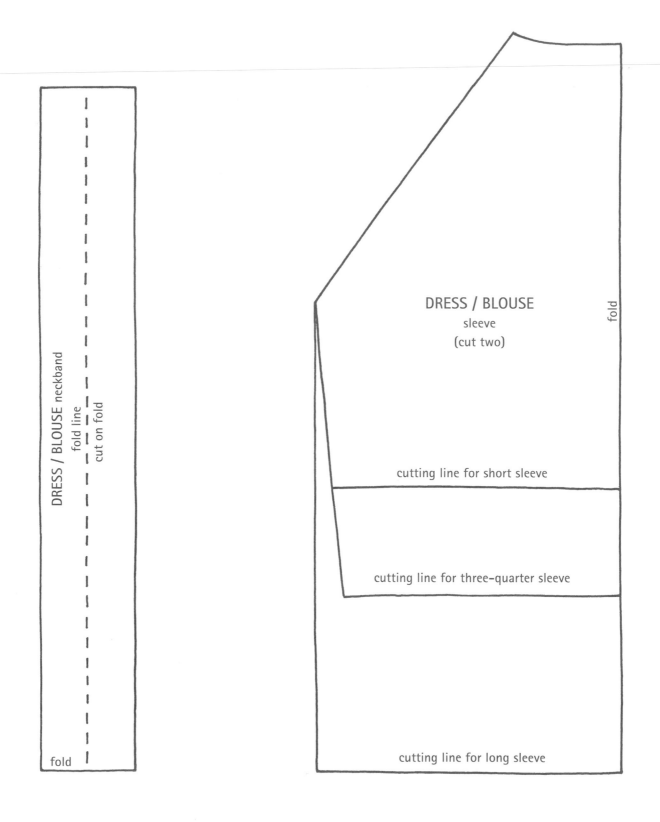

DRESS / BLOUSE neckband
fold line
cut on fold

fold

DRESS / BLOUSE
sleeve
(cut two)

fold

cutting line for short sleeve

cutting line for three-quarter sleeve

cutting line for long sleeve

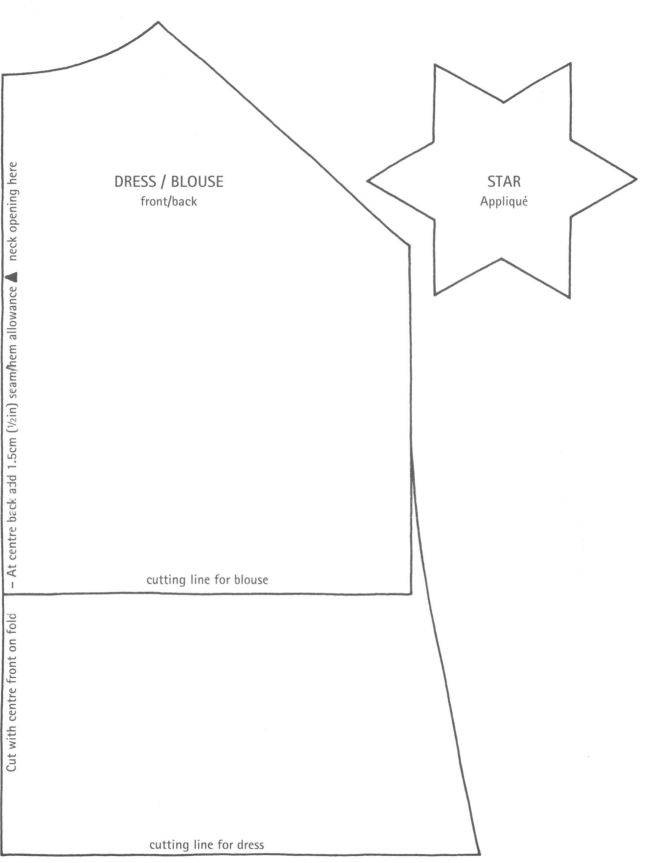

DRESS / BLOUSE
front/back

STAR
Appliqué

Cut with centre front on fold – At centre back add 1.5cm (½in) seam/hem allowance ◀ neck opening here

cutting line for blouse

cutting line for dress

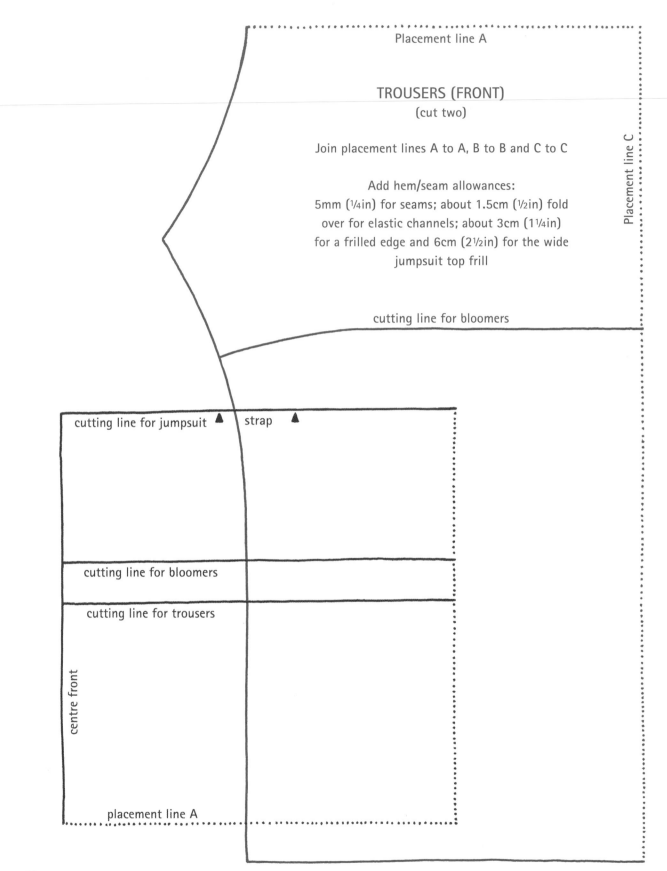

Placement line A

TROUSERS (FRONT)
(cut two)

Join placement lines A to A, B to B and C to C

Add hem/seam allowances:
5mm (¼in) for seams; about 1.5cm (½in) fold
over for elastic channels; about 3cm (1¼in)
for a frilled edge and 6cm (2½in) for the wide
jumpsuit top frill

Placement line C

cutting line for bloomers

cutting line for jumpsuit ▲ │ strap ▲

cutting line for bloomers

cutting line for trousers

centre front

placement line A

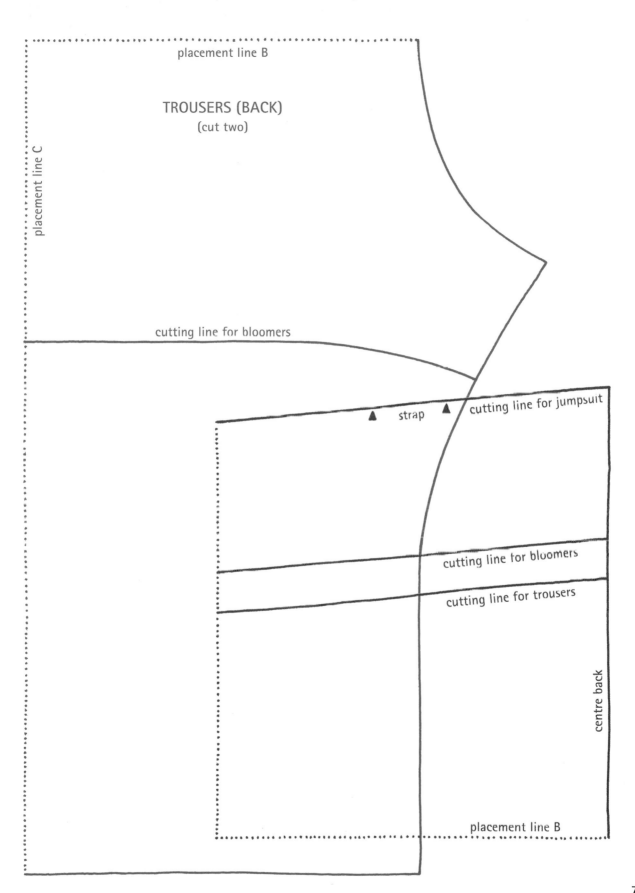

placement line B

TROUSERS (BACK)
(cut two)

placement line C

cutting line for bloomers

strap   cutting line for jumpsuit

cutting line for bloomers

cutting line for trousers

centre back

placement line B

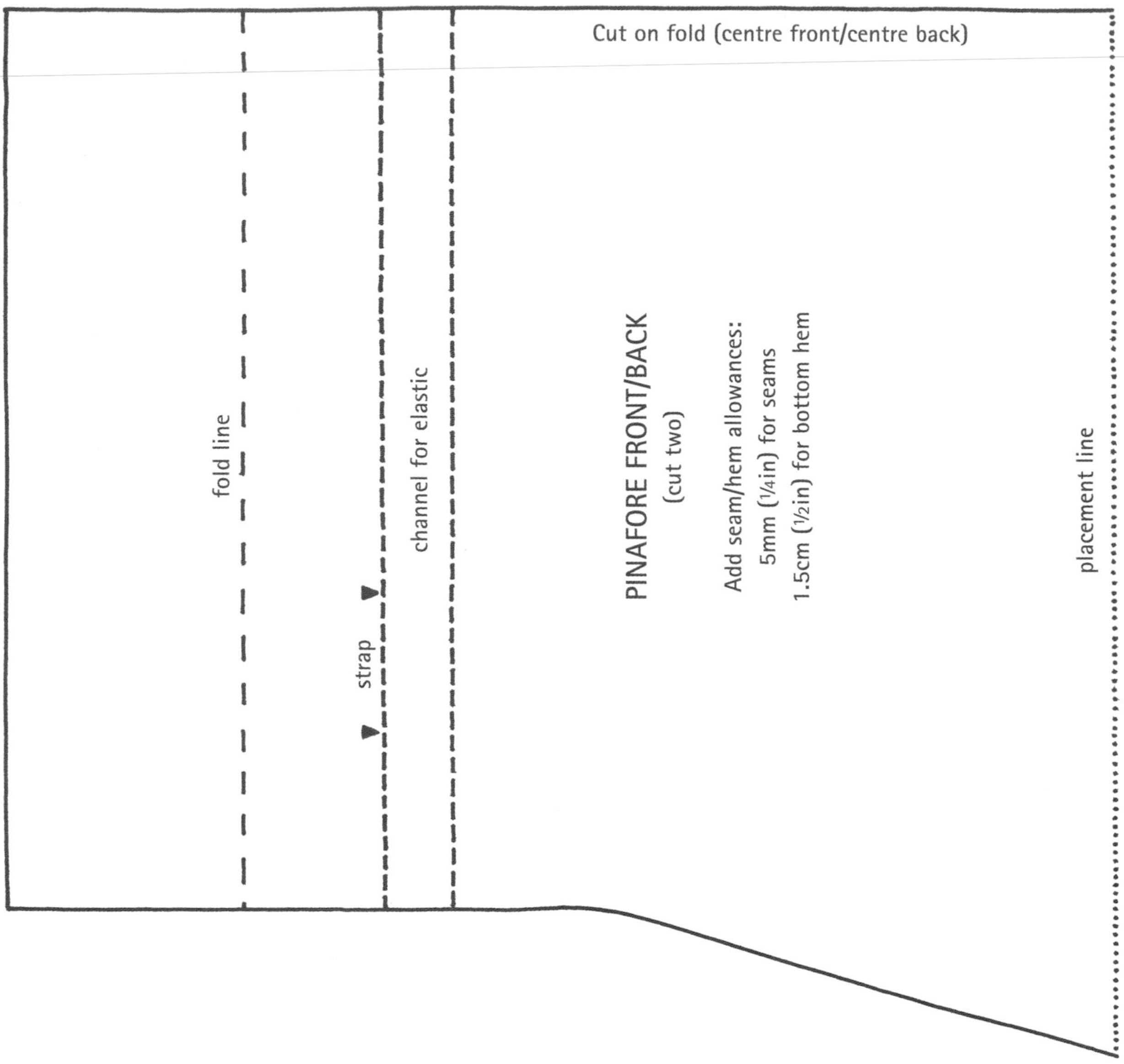

Cut on fold (centre front/centre back)

fold line

strap

channel for elastic

PINAFORE FRONT/BACK
(cut two)

Add seam/hem allowances:
5mm (¼in) for seams
1.5cm (½in) for bottom hem

placement line

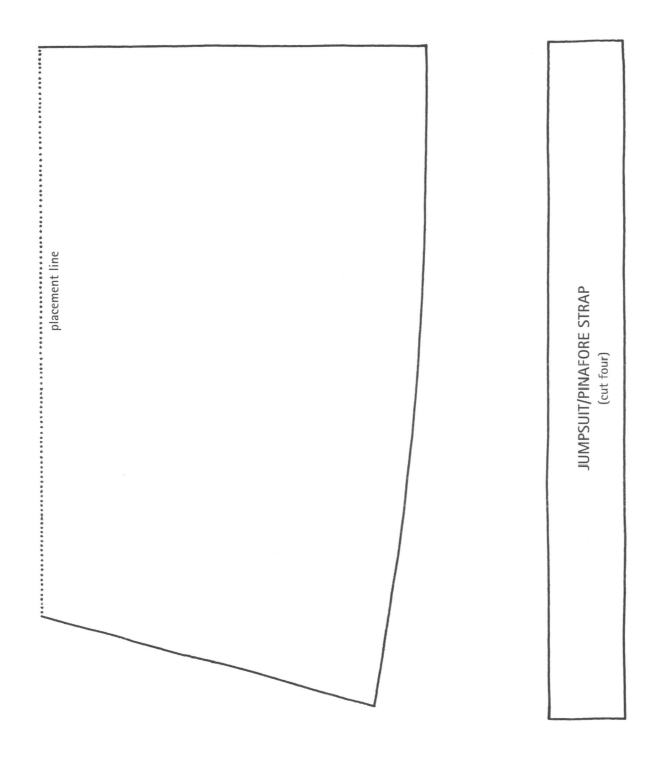

placement line

JUMPSUIT/PINAFORE STRAP
(cut four)

MATERIAL SUPPLIERS

The sources mentioned below refer to those organisations that supplied the materials and equipment used by the author. Many of these organisations provide on-line ordering facilities and distribute worldwide. However, all of the materials and equipment used in this book can be readily obtained from alternative sources, including specialist stores, on-line suppliers and mail-order companies.

For tubular gauze by the metre, tubular-knit doll fabric, wool stuffing, string, yarn for dolls' hair, Havblik cotton yarn and doll needles:

TANTE GRØN
Vestergade 7, 5000 Odense C
www.tantegroen.dk
Ph: +45 66 13 24 48

For embroidery supplies, including DMC embroidery cotton:

BRODERI MODERNE
Nørre Allé 45, 8000 Århus C
www.broderi-moderne.dk
Ph: +45 86 12 22 44

For embroidery supplies, including DMC embroidery cotton:

SOMMERFUGLEN
Vandkunsten 3, 1467 København K
www.sommerfuglen.dk
Ph. +45 33 32 82 90

For embroidery threads, knitting yarn and needlework supplies:

CREATIV COMPANY A/S
Rasmus Færchs Vej 23, 7500 Holstebro
www.cchobby.dk
Ph: +45 96 13 30 10

For embroidery threads, doll needles, knitting yarn and needlework supplies:

PANDURO HOBBY
www.pandurohobby.dk
Ph: +45 70 15 01 05